AGONY & ECSTASY

Reflections
Inspired by Our Lives

Edited by Jane E. Stahl & Sandra Williams

2013

Studio B

Edited by Jane E. Stahl and Sandra Williams
Book design by Susan Biebuyck
Volume One
Printed in 2013

———————————————

ISBN 978-0-9788838-4-3

Preface

Jane Stahl,
Director of Community Relations
Studio B

The inspiration: The exhibit "Agony and Ecstasy" was inspired by one of my favorite projects as a high school English teacher. Over the last five years of my career, my students and I "published" a series of books featuring their essays based on a reflective writing assignment I labeled "transforming moments."

For this assignment, I asked hundreds of sophomore honors students to write about a moment in their lives after which they were never the same. The essays that they presented and that we "published" in six volumes were incredibly thought-provoking and inspiring. I wanted the community to "meet" these wonderfully kind and sensitive, mature and intelligent human beings who showed up in my classroom. I figured folks should know the kinds of people their tax dollars were supporting!

The students and I distributed these books of essays as holiday gifts to each of their parents and members of our local school board. We placed books in beauty salons, doctors' offices, and libraries around our community.

Inspiration 2.0: After I retired from teaching, I became aware of a project called PostSecret. For this project, folks were asked to write a secret on a postcard anonymously and send it to the coordinator of the project. The response was robust. Hundreds of postcards subsequently became a series of PostSecret books and museum exhibits.

Reading the secrets was compelling and insightful. There could be no doubt: being human guarantees joy and sorrow, fear and anger. Reading the secrets—and recalling my students' essays--led me to conclude that becoming aware of our shared humanity should promote greater understanding, compassion, and tolerance of one another; inspire friendships; and ultimately create a stronger, more caring community.

Studio B—a Natural Fit: Since the mission of Studio B is designed to showcase the talents of visual and communication artists, this exhibit--combining literary and visual expressions--was a natural fit for our exhibition schedule. The exhibit includes a month-long show featuring visual art, poetry, and prose accompanied by a volume of the written submissions. The illustrations featured in this volume were generously donated by some of Studio B's most gifted artists.

Hope: I am hopeful that this effort serves as a way to share--not secrets, perhaps--but the wisdom that life imparts. There is no doubt: life is good and often difficult. We must celebrate our good times; and, in more challenging moments, hold hands and stick together!

Juror's Statement

Sandra Williams
Juror – Agony & Ecstasy Show

As a teacher of writing and literature for so many years, I am used to seeing, editing and revising all genres of writing from all ages and at all stages of a writer's development—from beginning composition to manuscripts for publication, which I suppose qualified me as a juror for the writing portion of this exhibit envisioned by Studio B: Agony & Ecstasy. I was enthusiastic to receive the writing submissions and eager to see how the show would take its final shape from that first envisioning.

The theme of Agony & Ecstasy was an inspiration for many to share the common experience of our sorrows and joys along life's path—and, as might have been expected, the agonies outweighed the ecstasies, not perhaps because life is so much more tragic, but rather that disillusionment, sadness, despair, fears, and tragedies can engender a depth of reflection, which some of us need to express in creative form, and which often serve to move us to another level of consciousness or way of being. Conversely, the height and light of our joys and ecstasies are savored in the moment and light up inwardly, often without need for reflection, analysis or expression. Still, these brighter moments are also opportunities for creativity, and they can and do offer affirmation and hope when they are shared.

Being a juror was quite an experience, which I am so pleased and honored to have had. Both the participation and the quality of the work submitted was more than I could have imagined. There is a broad range of writers represented: those who had never shared their writing before, as well as teachers of writing and published authors.

We have both agony and ecstasy eloquently and powerfully represented in this extraordinary show. I am grateful to have been part of such an endeavor and thank so very much the writers and artists for participating and sharing their contributions with the community for the Agony & Ecstasy show at Studio B.

Authors and Submissions

Preface..5

Juror's Statement 7

Ammon, Erik
A Tear of Remembrance.................................11

Barnett, Michael
This is Where I'm At.......................................13

Bennett, Craig H.
Nights on the Mountain (excerpt) 15

Benowitz, Sara
Morning – Night...19

Biebuyck, Susan
Crass #9 21

Bodien, Elizabeth
Two Pages Together.......................................23
Oksana Says Goodbye....................................24

Chisak, Mary
Two Haiku (A windswept wheat field and So many small suns)...26

Goodman, Heather
Raccoons 27

Joe Hoover
You Must Just Count to Seven 29

Keegan, Kathryn
Winter Solstice..31
Sunset at Summer Solstice 32

Klimcho, Marilyn L.T.
Complicated People 33
Chatting with Persephone.............................34

Klimcho, Patrick
Tough 36

Lupas, Jack
Trouble at the River 39

Mahony, Catherine
Translucent Portal 41
Green Tara 42

Misko, Lesley Huss
Subway Surfing 44

Peterson, Ellen
Conversation and Conversion on the Hill 47

Repko, Philip E.
Essence of Sentience 51
Vicarious Euphoria 52

Stahl, Jane
Family Matters 55
Haiku (It's spring) 56

Stehly, Burton
Bittersweet Vision 57
November 58
A Statement: Trauma 59

Tuck, Pamela M.
Missing Link 61

VanDyke, Diane
Lost Hopes 65
Parent Pride 66

White, Lauralynn
Forty-Four 69

Williams, Sandra
Ancient Injury 71

A Tear of Remembrance

Do you believe in love at first sight? I do. That's what happened when I met Sophia last night. She's just a friend of a friend whom I met when a bunch of us went out together after work. When we were introduced, a "Hi" formed on her lips, but no sound came out. She didn't need to say anything. The smile she gave and the look in her eyes said everything.

***

"I love you with all my heart. I want to spend every minute of every day with you. I want to be with you for all eternity," I proclaimed.

I watched Sophia's tears roll down her cheeks, to the edge of her chin, falling to the ground below.

"Will you marry me?" I asked.

"Do you even need to ask?" she sobbed. "Of course, Michael, of course I will."

***

I dreaded this night would happen. Michael's been flown in twice for a job interview in Houston. He called an hour ago. He was offered the job, and he's going to take it. I'm happy for him, but I'm still crying because I cannot go with him because of my job. This also means that we have to delay the wedding. I know we'll eventually get married, but I'm so upset. The wedding was supposed to be in three months. Michael's flying in tomorrow and then leaving the next day. He doesn't need to fly in; he just wants to say good-bye. He's such a romantic goof, and I can't wait to see him.

***

I heard a knock at the door. I assumed it was Michael. I answered it, smiling, ready to jump into his arms. When I opened the door, a police officer was standing there.

"Hello," he said, taking his hat off. "I have some horrible news," he said solemnly.

My heart sank. I knew what he was going to say. My tears fell like a rainy day downpour.

"Yes?" I said, my voice failing, betraying my feelings.

"Your fiance...he was...his plane crashed during landing." He was trying hard not to cry; I could tell by his choked, forced voice. "There weren't any survivors. I'm so sorry."

I don't remember much after that. I just sat down in the doorway and sobbed uncontrollably.

***

I don't remember how long I cried. Maybe for months, maybe even years. Whenever there was a knock at the door, I could only think of the moment I was told Michael was gone. Every time I closed my eyes, I saw him. Every time I slept, I dreamt of him, the good times, the bad, and his death. I'll never forget him nor ever stop loving him.

***

Sophia woke up in a cold sweat. Another nightmare. Another dream of what used to be, what could have been, but what never was to happen.

"What is it, honey?" her husband asked.

"Nothing," she replied. She laid her head back on her pillow, a tear streaming down her cheek.

Eric Ammon

Erik Ammon is a third-grade teacher, a long-distance running coach, and aspiring writer. He is currently working with an illustrator on a children's book, the third in his series, titled The Rabbit Who Wished He Could Fly, scheduled to be published in early 2014. One of his poems, published in the 90's based on the short story "Tear of Remembrance," appeared in an anthology entitled Carvings in Stone.

This is Where I'm At:

Within the sorrow of my despair

I watch my temple deteriorate

Then heal when I ask the Sun

To enter my sacred space

Glorious golden-yellow rays

Illuminate every cell in my body

The passionate energy of the Universe

Calls my name and resonates with

Sonorous tones which defy gravity,

Soothe my ears, speak from my tongue,

And cause my being

To vibrate with unbounded fertility

My breath eases, my gait lengthens,

And I feel the presence of God.

© 2013 Michael Barnett

Rev. Michael Barnett, M. Div., M. Ed., works as an interfaith minister and counselor, educator, and teaching artist/poet. He earned his Master of Divinity Magna Cum Laude at Moravian Theological Seminary and his Master of Education Master Teacher from Gwynedd-Mercy College where he taught religious studies.

For twelve years, Michael has spoken and taught on the Transcendentalists Emerson, Margaret Fuller, and Unitarian minister Theodore Parker. He teaches workshops on intuition, sacred marriage, and intuitive tarot. Michael's spiritual poetry and articles are published in literary and religious journals. He has served as a teaching artist in poetry with the Lehigh Valley Arts Council's Urban/Suburban Afterschool Arts Program, the Santa Fe Children's Museum, and the Montgomery County Poetry WITS program. Michael weaves rag rugs and paints abstract watercolors and acrylics which have been exhibited in the Moravian Theological Seminary meditation room, the U.S. Attorney's Office in Philadelphia, the first AIDS exhibition at the Painted Bride Center, Philadelphia, and in the traveling exhibition In Response to Healing.

Excerpt from
NIGHTS ON THE MOUNTAIN: A
SPIRITUAL JOURNEY

After he had finished his dinner and carefully buried the refuse, he was ready to turn in. He'd filled his water bottles again not long ago, and he wanted to boil up a batch to let cool overnight so that he wouldn't have to put one of those godawful-tasting iodine tablets into it. But he wasn't sure that he'd be able to stay awake that long. He could see the first few stars of evening just becoming visible overhead. The air was still chilly, but it seemed a little less damp than it had earlier in the day.

He sat down on one of the logs near the fire pit and looked up at the sky remembering other times on other mountains when he had looked up at the fall of evening and marveled at what lay spread out above him. It was so different from what he was accustomed to seeing back home. There the humidity, the various pollutants that hung in the air, and the ambient light from a hundred different sources reduced the number of visible stars in the sky by a factor he had no way of calculating; but he knew that the number had to be large. Here, on the other hand, the heavens were alive with stars, spread like the dust of diamonds across a sky of pure obsidian.

The air was pure and cool, too, scented just enough with the smell of damp earth and evergreen forest. Everything he could see from where he sat was clean, fresh, and unsullied by human activity. No trash, no litter, no graffiti, no dirt and grime, no pollution. And there was silence. Only an occasional breeze caressing the limbs of trees at the edge of the surrounding forest made a faint, transient, barely audible sound. And he was alone—alone with his thoughts, his memories, his longings, and his dreams. This, he reminded himself, was why he loved mountains. This was why he sought them out to begin with and why he kept returning to them whenever he could. And as he sat in the silence of the evening, looking up at the incredibly rich scattering of stars across the heavens, he was reminded of something else that had compelled him to seek out mountains. They had called to him through music, as well.
**

The summer after he graduated from college he had bought a recording of songs in the folk idiom by Béla Bartók and Zoltán Kodály, two twentieth-century Hungarian composers with whose orchestral

music he was already somewhat familiar. The music was performed
by the Kodály Girls' Chorus of Budapest, a group of young girls from
eight to thirteen years of age whose voices were as pure and clear as the
ringing of crystal bells. And the second track on the album was a piece
by Kodály called "Nights on the Mountain: A Wordless Song."

Illustration by Lauralynn White

There were a few pieces of music that had an immediate and profound
effect on him the first time he heard them. The primitive, driving
rhythms of Stravinsky's "Rite of Spring." The magnificent sweep of
Sibelius' second symphony. The lush sensuality of Ravel's "Daphnis and
Chloe." But this short, wordless song, sung with such resonant purity
by those young girls from Budapest, moved him as few things had
before or since. It was an incredibly effective evocation of something
that he had in fact never really experienced. If one could imagine
music that would recall the gentle falling of snow from a leaden sky, or
the lazy drifting of autumn leaves through the crisp, dry twilight air,
then one could imagine the nature of Kodály's song.

Only many years later, watching the gradual fading of the pale
orange alpenglow from a mountainside far above Sion in the Swiss
Alps, would he realize how right Kodály was. For as the sky slowly gave
way to night, filling up with more stars than he had any idea existed
within the range of human eyesight, this was what he heard: Kodály's
wordless song. It was in the sound of the wind moving easily among
the high ridges, brushing the forested shoulders of the mountain. It

was in the occasional plaintive call of a bird settling into its nest amid the growing silence of the night. It was in the gentle lowing of the fuzzy, brown Alpine cattle as they lay down on the same soft grass they had browsed all through the brilliant mountain day. It was in the ringing of his ears, the coursing of blood through his veins, the sound of his own body's unobtrusive functioning that becomes apparent only when the surrounding silence is so deep, so profound, so absolute that the surface tension of thought is subtly broken, and a mind at peace with itself and in reverent awe of its surroundings quietly begins to sing.

Craig H. Bennett

From: <u>Nights on the Mountain: A Spiritual Journey</u>, *available at www. amazon.com and www.barnesandnoble.com, and at selected book stores, on Kindle and from the author*

Craig's background includes stints as a musician, an on-camera and voice-over performer, and a part-time art student at PCA and PAFA, as well as a teacher of English. He has recently begun work on a second book based on his participation in a 1984 expedition into northeastern Brazil on the trail of Col. Percival H. Fawcett, who disappeared in 1925 while searching for the ruins of an ancient city he designated as "Z."

Craig is interested in classical music, literature, travel (especially Western Europe), maverick archaeology, and the eternal questions that have stumped philosophers for ages. He welcomes the opportunity to discuss these things with anyone who shares an interest in them.

Morning

Bright, dreams aswhirl:
Anything is possible.
I'm such a lucky girl:
Feeling unstoppable.

Rested, I feel power:
The future is grabable.
Day's finest hour;
By night, my goals laughable.

Night

Morning's glow now black:
Dreams faded fast.
Hopes early, dashed:
Thinking of the past.

Mourning what I lack:
Foibles amassed.
Oblivion, at last:
Sleep brings morning back.

Sara Benowitz

Sara Benowitz is a writer and visual artist, as well as an academic tutor. Her written work has appeared in literary journals and media. A proud member of Studio B and The Dumpster Divers of Philadelphia, her often environmentally-conscious artwork has been featured in a South Street gallery and regional shows, including one she curated in her current hometown of Ambler, PA.

Crass the Cat
by Susan Biebuyck

Crass #9

His heart slipped into sadness created by the loss of Crass. In the shower, awash in tears and warmth, mud dripped slowly from his hands. He didn't want to erase too soon the last touch of his fur. His DNA remained while the water, mud, blood, a few hairs dripped from his fingertips. He knew they would never grace his hand again. He stood there naked, crying, hiding from his wife, bathing in sadness. She loved Crass too, but, still, over the years, Norm had never shown that depth of emotion to her about the cat. They shared feelings, but it was his husbandly duty to protect her from pain. Crass knew Norman's feelings and would purr at the sight of him.

Only minutes earlier, Norman Wells, driving home, noticed the lump on the road. Slowing, he hoped it would move out of the way. He could see the lump was going nowhere. It wasn't all there – half smear, half body – but he recognized the fur.

Norman jumped into action. Knowing Jane was on her way home, he left the car in the road, retrieved the body, and moved it to a spot in the backyard. He laid Crass on the warm grass. He wasn't crying yet. No, he was in man-of-the-house mode. His job was to dig the grave. He focused on it.

Rummaging through the shed, he found a dull shovel and began the task of removing turf. A foot down, he hit rock. Feeling urgency, he moved closer to Jane's zinnia bed. "Yeah," he told himself, "she'll want to visit Crass too. We'll put him here near Jane's flowers." Then he heard his own voice and realized that the shock of what he was doing was making him talk out loud to himself.

Inches deep, another unmanageable rock. Norman was perplexed. Already a blister and precious minutes into the gruesome task, he knew he must hurry.

Months earlier, he'd tilled the soil for Jane's flower bed. Remembering the pain of removing boulders with a pickaxe, he recalled Crass peeing in the loam shortly after seeds were planted, another secret from Jane. Now flowers were in full bloom.

"I wonder," thought Norman, "if I dig carefully keeping the roots intact...." Norman slid the shovel next to the zinnias. He laid them on the grass beside Crass, a lump of soil with brightly colored flowers embedded in it.

Hurrying, digging soft soil, Norman created a grave for Crass's mangled body. He gently laid it in the warm August soil about four feet down, hopefully deep enough. Touching where he thought the heart was, Norm said a prayer about how great a cat Crass was, remembered finding him as a kitten, recalled when Jane had the baby and Crass felt left out, and the guilt from the time they went away for the weekend and forgot to leave food. Then there was that time Crass delivered a dead bunny through the cat door and Norman had to dispose of that body, too.

Quickly filling in the hole, Norman dusted the grass clean. He patted the base of the flowers, finishing with some of the compost from last spring.

It wasn't until he put away the shovel and headed back to park the car that Crass's death gripped him. In the shower, he let it go down the drain. The water warmed his body. Shampoo, then soap; he was starting to feel clean. Ring, ring – the phone.

Off with the water, grabbing a towel, he raced to beat the answering machine. It was Jane. She was picking up pizza and wanted to know if he wanted beer.

"Norman, is everything okay?" She'd detected a note in his voice.

"Yes. Jane. I'll set the table for pizza and beer. See you shortly."

Dressing, he thought about how he would tell Jane after a beer or two. Heading to the kitchen, burdened with protecting Jane, he grabbed a tablecloth from the linen closet and headed downstairs. Norman ran into the kitchen and most naturally where you'd expect to see him, right in the middle of the table sat Crass the cat, healthy and alive.

"Meow."

Susan Biebuyck

*S*usan is a full-time working artist however, "nurturing the collective intellect" is behind her role as Gallery Director & Curator of Studio B. Since the opening of Studio B, Susan has welcomed hundreds of artists, patrons and community members to a variety of exhibits. As an artist, Susan's own work has been sold in national and international collections, received numerous awards, and exhibited throughout the U.S. and Europe. Her work promises amusement in its variety of subjects. She is drawn to energy, nourishment, connectivity and decadence — landscapes always dotted by power lines which keep us connected to one another, the ever-common nourishment of FOOD and its enticement. Her solo shows are often theme-based featuring a common thread or idea that knits a collection together and allows her to explore many techniques, styles, supplies, colors and theories. She refers to herself as an "art supplies junky." Her mission in creating is to have fun.

Two Pages Together

Such emerald greens,
rich reds, royal blues
in the storybook Bible.
Then that one scary picture.
I knew where it was,
each time would skip over it,
turn two pages together
not to see the dark chamber
with windowless walls,
figures leaning and wailing.
More grimacing figures
leaned down through a hole,
a square hole in the ceiling,
their skeletal arms
stretched down in need,
the tumult of bodies
in ragged affliction.
A child would want
no part of that scene.
Now it's your suffering
I want to make vanish,
cast out your torment
from that shuttered room,
fetid with hurt,
you sleeping away
from your torn apart world.
You cannot move

to whatever is next.

I would open a window,

invite in fresh air, turn two pages together

to banish this picture -- you in that pit,

so deep and so tangled

my arms extended

to you cannot reach.

Elizabeth Bodien

Oksana Says Goodbye

My handgrip loosens on the metal bar.
My reflexes have slowed. It's time to quit.
Lucky me, no big catastrophes.
But acrobats can't twist and fly forever.

It's tricky to know the best time to retire.
My health is good but eyesight's getting worse.
One needs the vision of a hungry Strix
to see the wires when tent lights go to dim.

I'll miss my slinky, sequined costumes
and when the people gasp -- one huge breath.
After such spectacular creations,
I wonder where I'll hear applause again.

The hotel life I gladly leave to others.
That lost its appeal decades ago,
exciting when I was an eager girl
showing off, the spotlight bright and warm.

My daughter will not take up the trapeze.
She'll choose a safer way to live, I hope.
But what a thrill it was each time the men
would swing through air, like birds, to grab me tight—

the pumping beat, the contact, and release,
the beauty of our bodies in their joy.
What thrills the audience felt could never match
the ecstasy of soaring at the heights.

Elizabeth Bodien

*E*lizabeth Bodien lives near Hawk Mountain, PA. Her degrees are in cultural anthropology, consciousness studies, and the history and phenomenology of religion from the University of California, John F. Kennedy University, and the Graduate Theological Union. She has worked as an English teacher in Japan, an organic farmer in the coastal mountains of Oregon, a childbirth instructor in West Africa, and a Montessori teacher in California. Her poems have appeared in The Fourth River, Frogpond, Mad Poets Review, Schuylkill Valley Journal, Cimarron Review, Qarrtsiluni, and U.S.1 Worksheets, among other publications in the United States, Canada, Australia, Ireland, and India. Her collections are in the award-winning chapbook, Plumb Lines; Rough Terrain: Notes of an Undutiful Daughter; and Endpapers.

Crows Rising
by Jillian Prout

A windswept wheat field
gathers heavy clouds and crows
the bright crimson flows.

Mary Chisak

So many small suns
the empty canvas holds
ecstasy of gold!

Mary Chisak

Mary Chisak, usually participates in the visual arts, but she has loved poetry since she was a child and has begun expressing herself also through this art form. She became interested in the poetic form of Haiku through Sumi-e ink painting, which often includes Haiku poetry as part of the painting's composition expressed in beautiful flowing calligraphy.

Raccoons

The raccoons, a mother and her young, came the night of the letter, howling and screeching. They'd figured out the lock on the smokehouse door. Only a simple turn of a wooden handle, but the animals had never broken in before, and the meat was wasted. They'd climbed chinked walls, torn venison from shelves. What they hadn't gnawed, they'd covered in ash, tossed to the coals, annihilating even this little bit of something.

Mac caught them, one at a time, for six nights straight. He used the same Havahart trap he employed for pests even his family wouldn't eat, capturing one adult and five teenagers. Instead of releasing them as he'd done before being drafted, he put them, one each morning, in a trash can, dropped in a rag soaked in ether, and clamped the lid on the can. He sat on a log and waited, crutches beside him, plaster of paris cast extended before him, not cleaning his shotgun, not sharpening knives, not ordering supplies for the family smoked meat business, not anything.

When each raccoon stopped thrashing, nails no longer gouging, tail no longer thwapping, Mac removed the lid and dumped the can upside down. From the tin of ether, he dampened another rag, inhaling its chemical smell of magic markers and glass cleaner. He reached under the garbage can and pulled out the stunned raccoon. The ether in the trash can would have killed the varmint, but Mac cradled the animal anyway, a rag to its face. An unnecessary step. Like the army. He could have gotten out, maybe. At least applied for a marriage deferment. But then he would have been forced to stay— would have been locked in. To June. To the baby. To a business he never had a chance to leave.

When June let him put his hand on her bulging belly, he'd called the baby "Hero" to complete the illusion Mac had been saved. He'd continued the sham until the letter.

Just three weeks since his would-have-been unit arrived in the jungle, Mac ripped open the air mail envelope, surprised and pleased Eddie thought of him. Eddie's words, all slanted caps on paper nearly as thin as tissue, spelled out his reason for writing: Dimestore and Bibs were dead. Eddie's script rankled: "That jeep was the best damn thing that ever happened to you."

Now, for the sixth night in a row, he kneeled, covered a raccoon's face, damp dirt bleeding into Mac's knees, the smell of autumn soil—weak and closing down—in his lungs until the ether wafted to him. The young raccoon, too small this late into fall, no larger than a rabbit, didn't move, the ether potent. But the animal's body was still warm, and when Mac palmed its grey shape, he felt its nascent bones, its still weight. With the white handkerchief, he covered the raccoon's pointed nose, bent the silken whiskers, saw his reflection in its onyx eyes, and recognized who he'd meant to be.

Heather Goodman, 2013

Heather E. Goodman grew up in the woods of Pennsylvania where her family raised raccoons, opossums, kids, and dogs. Her fiction has been published in Gray's Sporting Journal, Hunger Mountain, The Crab Orchard Review, Minnesota Monthly, and the Chicago Tribune, where her story "His Dog" won the Nelson Algren Award. Heather notes that "'Raccoons' is an excerpt from my novel, which partly examines my obsession with the fact that my parents were married before Vietnam and spent their early dating/married years fighting the draft, then ultimately dealing with basic and AIT, and then the long, long months while my dad served as a medic in Vietnam."

You Must Just Count to Seven

Hoover paint to poetry?
Now, that is a big challenge!
The final decision was
that, first, I paint the picture;
then, write verse to explain it.
Of course, I'm not a poet,
But, if you study these lines,
You will notice that each one
Contains seven syllables.
That's my justification:
At least the rhythm is there.

But why do I choose seven?
Well, my daily mailbox walks
are done to seven beat count:
LEFT right left right left right left;
RIGHT left right left right left right.
(Think: Ole Joe Has Gone Fishing:
Ben Britten wrote that chorus
Seven beats per each measure.)

But that's all about this verse.
Let's talk about the painting.
Having no verse to portray,
I simply threw on colors.
Yes, "threw" is aptly chosen--
Primaries red, yellow, blue.

You say you cannot see them?
Well, in the beginning stage
you could distinguish them all,
but the effect was not good.
Emotion soon took over.

Though the second-hand frame
did not deserve much better,
I took hold of a big brush,
filled it with white acrylic,
and frustration took command.

Finally, a blowing fan
caught the paint's many drippings
and helped bring this masterpiece
to its seven count finish.

Joe Hoover

There has always been a strong connection with art throughout Joe's life: childhood coloring books, teenage pastel paintings, elementary classroom teacher bulletin board displays, and seasonal greeting cards, as well as program cover designs and posters during his choral conducting career. But it was soon after retirement twenty years ago that art became Joe's main focus. Now, with memberships in art organizations and galleries in the Boyertown, Reading, Pottstown, and West Chester areas, his annual calendar includes more than two dozen art shows (juried, non-juried, group, and solo). Watercolor remains his medium of choice in creating florals, still lifes, landscapes, and abstracts.

Winter Solstice

Slumber
by Lauralynn White

On the shortest day
I walk in search of solace
The leafless trees were mute
Silenced in the frozen landscape.

The laws of return
Buried deep in the heartwood
Guarantees that light returns

In this world of guns and hate
Greed and glut
 This is the comfort I need -
 the promise that days of growing Light
heed the sacred code

Kathryn Keegan

Sunset on the Summer Solstice

Lavender wings
ease
solstice fire
onto tidal marsh.

This sunset lasts
until
the melting point
vanishes somewhere
beyond hazed grasses.

Even marsh life
teeming with wild things
holds still
until
the hallowed moment passes.

This longest day
retreats
and I am content
to watch the passing
until
last light.

Kathryn Keegan, 2007

Kathryn Keegan is a poet and artist living in Birchrunville, Chester County, PA. She creates works that evoke a world of timeless patterns through observations of nature. Her poems are rooted in gratitude and awe. At times her poetry discloses her spiritual unrest for the human condition and its frailities. Meanwhile she pursues her search one poem at a time.

Complicated People

I know people
As complicated
And as frantic as
Knots in shoe laces
When battery acid
Splashes on work pants,
As intricate as embroidery
Or lace from Brussels.

I know people
As oblivious to
The complex ones
As the discs of harrows
That furrow open nests of baby field mice.

Sometimes the two kinds of people
Live with each other.

Marilyn L.T. Klimcho, 2010

Chatting with Persephone

On the phone
You sound so happy.
Overjoyed is not too strong
A word.
Thrilled to be back
In your own home at ninety-three
For one more spring and summer.

But each time
After you leave my house
And I clean up the guest bedroom…
Find toothpicks you dropped after a meal,
Tissues you tucked under
Your pillow at night,
Tablets that escaped
Your fingers when
You replenished
Your pillbox each Sunday,
Move on to the kitchen and find…
The package of Red Rose teabags
You forgot to pack,
The jar of seedless raspberry jelly
I forgot to send along…

Each time you
Return to your home for the summer, it's
A mini-death for me and

I am cast as Hades,

Ruler of the Underworld,

Your abductor for the winter

When all I meant to do

Was a daughter's duty:

To love and

Keep you safe.

Is this what it will feel like

When we bury your

Ancient body?

Marilyn L.T. Klimcho, 2013

Marilyn Klimcho is a short story writer and poet who grew up in Susquehanna County in Northeastern Pennsylvania. Marilyn serves as treasurer of Berks Bards, Inc., a grassroots group dedicated to nourishing the living art of poetry in Berks County. Her work has appeared in the Schuylkill Valley Journal *and she has received a nomination for a Pushcart Prize.*

Tough

It was twenty-five years this May,
A quarter- century. . . .
I keep track by my daughter's age.
She was six months old when he died.
I saw him hold her just one time.

He was a pisser!
Bone and sinew—
Squint and gimp . . .
All the so-called tough guys called 'him' by name
With a respect the anonymous "sir" couldn't muster.

Those sly, black eyes
Could look inside your head,
And his gaunt cheek would crease
In the faintest suggestion of a smile,
Companionably silent.

He was hard, yet generous,
Taciturn but a great storyteller.
His tales always funny
In a scary sort of way.
Baseball was his religion.

Twenty-five years gone. . .
Fifty-six years here. . .
Four lost in a hospital bed,
His back broken at seventeen,
Paralyzed, he thought, forever.

But the Army surgeons put him back together,
Or he was too damned stubborn to give up.
Read it your way.
His feet began to burn when the nerves reconnected,
And they cut away his plaster home that stretched from chest to
     ankles.

They propped what was left of his skinny carcass
Against the wall and told him to stand.
His wasted legs gave way,
And he slowly slid down that white painted wall
Until a Doctor's sharp right to the gut straightened those legs.

He stood
Stood up to a steel mill for thirty-two years
Had a family and glued it together,
Cried, just once, when his little sister died.
It was an honor to put my hand on his shoulder.

They talk about "tough."
But we don't know "tough."
I haven't seen "tough"
In twenty-five years.

Patrick Klimcho, 2007

*P*atrick Klimcho is a novelist and poet who grew up in Phoenixville, a steel town in Southeastern Pennsylvania. Patrick has a knack for and enjoys writing parodies. He equates it to the challenge of doing crosswords. Patrick has published poetry in the Schuylkill Valley Journal and Up and Under: the QND Review. He resides in Reading with his wife of thirty-four years.

Agony
by Judy Lupas

Trouble at the River

My brother Tony, age 7, and I, age 9, were visiting my aunt and uncle in a town near Sunbury, Pennsylvania in 1942. When we got to her house she told us about a surprise. "It"s a trip with a young minister from our church," she said. "He will take you for a ride in his row boat for a picnic and swim!"

Tony and I loved the water. We jumped up and down and said "Let"s go!" The day arrived and we went to the river. The minister told us to call him Jim. Jim's boat was there at the water's edge. We jumped into the boat and Jim paddled out. He told us this was a shallow part. I jumped into the water and swam out a little to show off. Tony didn't know how to swim yet.

Jim said, "Jump in and move your arms and legs like your brother." My brother was a little anxious, but he showed Jim the swimming strokes. Jim jumped into the water and Tony slid over the side into the water to Jim.

Then Jim said, "Try to swim!"

Tony said, "I can"t swim yet! Put me back in the boat!" He began to whimper.

Jim said, "Come on, Tony. You should be swimming by now!" He picked up Tony and held him under his abdomen and said, "Now move your arms and legs!" As he let go of my brother, I saw Tony start to sink under the surface of the water.

I screamed, "He went under! What if he drowns? Help, help!" There was a fisherman nearby who came over to see what was going on. He and Jim lifted my brother into the boat. Tony looked blue and was having trouble breathing and began to cough. I was crying. As soon as Tony could breath better, he started to swing his arms and punch Jim.

You tried to kill me!" Jim reached for Tony, pulled him close and tried to kiss him on the cheek. I felt that wasn't right. The fisherman told him that it was a bad thing to do, letting him go under

the water when he couldn't swim.
"You better take them home now!" said the fisherman.

When we got home we told my aunt what happened. "We are not going again. He tried to kill Tony!" I said. My aunt said we were supposed to go three times, and that the minister would be angry if we didn't. "You don't know what happened! We are not going and we want to go home now!" We called our parents and they came the next day.

We still talk about that day that Tony almost drowned. I wonder what it would have been like to have grown up without a brother.

Jack Lupas

Jack Lupas is a published poet, who grew up in a working class family in the coal region of Pennsylvania. He retired after forty-five years of practicing family medicine. Jack has written poetry all through his life and recently gathered his poems in the book entitled, The Ferris Wheel. He has studied this craft at local colleges and writes often of the lives he has observed, embellished with his imagination. Jack lives with his wife of 35 years and enjoys his children and grandchildren. A fellow poet said that he represents "a life well lived." Jack says he wants to write a memoir. Those who know him agree!

Translucent Portals

An Ekphrastic poem depicting Laura Gelsomini's "Seeds of Change" (Illustated on Page 46)

Ivory bonnet defiled by ash,

All-knowing eyes gaze into the hereafter.

Garbed in a yellow sheath of hope and unscathed joy,

An innocent reflects upon a journey taken not so long ago.

Gateways known only in dreams, left ajar in a single expression.

Tiny palms of a cherub pressed delicately upon a pain;

Imprinted liquid solidified to confine.

Dwelling on an alternate plateau,

naïve to guttural roars.

Icebound vehemence suspended amidst two worlds.

Moans of apparitions not yet made clamor in the backdrop –

Echoing, muffled screams trapped in innocent lungs.

Anticipation of a fictional execution sets the stage for

actuated fatalities.

Translucent portals sever an inextinguishable yearning to survive.

Wombs that carried a town to prosperity desecrated by embers-

Their recent occupants drown in a sea of embryonic flame as well.

Disembodied terror splits atoms with strokes of purple and

crimson.

Frigid blues and scorching reds procreate violet energy

As they labor to bring forth a balance between body and soul.

Visages once recognizable by loved ones

Liquefy like wax dissipating from a half- spent candle.

Nebulae conjure in a peaceful cobalt sky to transport souls from the

horrific scene.

Energies gather in-between smoky polluted particles to reunite in
    illuminating purity.
Some will remain as a residual reminder – to carry the burden –
    as heavy and cumbersome as the pane upon which this tragedy
    was recomposed in a flash of somber inspiration.

Catherine Mahony

Green Tara

An Ekphrastic poem depicting Laura Gelsomini's "Bowl 49"

Alms bowls provide empty spaces within-a receptacle for unwanted
desires and lustful things.
    No need for glitter or gold and all the pain such things bring.
    The forty-ninth is claimed, by a woman who floats near the Bodhi
tree, after divine ducts conjure rain.
    Her consciousness drifts in a shimmering puddle born from tears
of compassion-
    From Buddha- who wept over a world riddled with suffering.
    Her epidermal sheath elongates across the latitude of a diamond-
shaped canvas-
    Lapis Lazuli eyes engorge and absolve the cessation of suffering for
her viewers.
    Beams of light from above assist the lotus in bloom, as it sprouts
fleshy appendages meant to loom.
    Blue blouse symbolizes intellectual life.
    Staring askew, contemplating Universal strife.
    Green Tara's white skirt purifies spirit and mind-with the smelting

of metal and the extreme cold of snow.

Goddess of knowledge longs to share what she holds;

A gift reciprocated by an act of detachment, a bowl tossed away after dividing its contents.

Colorful containers just as temporal as their craftsman, represent borrowed flesh from the days before Eden.

Bodies, souls and minds strive to remain neutral, less engaged with things that allure them, longing to fill a void with purified fruit from an impure garden.

Pottery spindle products manufactured in hues of green and blue,

Begging bowls separated and dispersed, scattered about the reflective room.

The Goddess has chosen the final piece in the collection, in hopes she will attain enlightenment by way of her own reflection.

Detach from all worldly objects and return to the core.

Choose Bowl 49 and be whole once more.

Catherine Mahony

Catherine Mahony, originally from New York, is a creative writer of all genres. She was recently published in Legacy a literary journal, and was this year's recipient of annual Reading Area Community College Creative Writing award. As a full time student, she enjoys being a correspondent for the Front Street Journal, the two-year college's newspaper. She is not afraid to tackle controversial issues, such as homosexuality, addiction and mental illness—feeling that when the proper amount of light is shed on these topics–healing can begin. Her inspiration for her ekphrastic poetry was the looming talent of artist Laura Gelsomini. Ms. Mahony related deeply to Mrs. Gelsomini's artwork, which evokes intense emotion. What she connected to most was Gelsomini's fearless approach, as she is not afraid to paint off the "beaten path." Cat "Mahony thoroughly enjoyed painting a portrait with words that was already so beautifully mastered with a brush.

Subway Surfing

I used to surf the New York subways,
    seemingly smoothly gliding
        over miles of silver metal track,
            as the baby blue train car,
        a gift of the '64 World's Fair,
        careened its way around curves.

    It was my surfboard,
seemingly bouncing off the concrete walls
    that kept the track imprisoned,
        jolting to an abrupt STOP
            in each of the brightly tiled stations,
        also baby blue.

    No overhead straps for me.
And I shunned the shiny metal poles
    that grew from the tile floors
        like artificial mushrooms.

            Instead, legs spread w -i -d -e
                to create a new center of gravity,
            my body twisted rhythmically,
        to take the curves
    in stride, as each one came.
Even at mid-day,
    when the cars were nearly empty,
        I disdained the seats,

a few claimed by tired women

with their endlessly chatty children

or by unmemorable men working odd shifts.

I was young and sturdy,

and I yearned to ride the waves of steel,

sharp eyes searching out the distant skyline

as the train car

lu- rch- ed,

ever closer to my destination.

My surfing days are over.

Back and knees hurting now,

it is of no comfort to recall

the skill I once had,

as I gingerly crawl into cabs.

Lesley Huss Misko

*L*esley grew up surfing the New York City subways and loving the freedom and accessibility they provided to all that the city offered. After earning a BA in English from Queens College, City University of New York (CUNY), and an MS in English Education from Syracuse University, Misko spent 35 years teaching 11th and 12 grade English. In addition to chairing the Boyertown Area Senior High English Department and advising the award-winning high school newspaper, both for 15 years, Misko was active in scholastic journalism at the state and national levels, directed senior class plays, advised the National Honor Society, and chaired the school's program for gifted students. She currently writes for Pottstown.Patch.com. A resident of Gilbertsville, she is married to Robert, has a son, Sean, and two cats, Barry and Fiona.

Seeds of Change
by Laura Gelsomini, 2012

(Poetry for this illustration on page 41.)

Conversation and Conversion on the Hill

I was visiting my mother's and father's gravesites, a habit I'd developed as a substitute for driving aimlessly whenever I needed to escape from my husband and one or both of my children.

The cemetery was on a steep hill, just outside of town where you could look out over the small community that my mother loved and refused to leave for longer than a week at a time. Living in Burlington was a condition of their marital contract. There was no way my mother would consider moving from her beloved town.

In those days, Dad would agree to any demands; he adored her, but knew he was perhaps fourth on her list of VIP's. He figured he followed me, my brother, and our beagle in any competitive race for her affections.

Sometimes I looked for four-leaf clovers while I worried on the hill; other times I searched the panorama to catch a glimpse of the roofline of my family home between the trees—the half-double my daughter now occupies but the one I hate to visit now that Mom and Dad have "relocated."

Today I found myself talking out loud…to myself…or so I thought. I had some serious worries about my son; some serious frustrations with my husband of 40 years; and an undying grief about my daughter, grief that accompanies the death of a dream for her health and happiness and our family's wholeness. As my sister-in-law once said, "Your family is so f_____ up." She was right. Today the silent guardians of that hill heard all of our family's ugly secrets. I needed to tell someone of my fears and heartache.

My monologue was broken by a gravely baritone: "What's your problem, Ellen?"

Surprised to hear a voice that was not my own, I stuttered, "Wha…Who are…" but was quickly silenced when the gentleman chuckled, offering, "Oh, nevermind; that was a rhetorical question. I already know what troubles you." He chuckled, again. "I'm omniscient, as you know."

I stood, backing up slowly down the hill toward my car and this time finished the query: "Who are you?"

"Just call me GD," he offered. "I'm trying to be 'hip' this decade, and I understand that using two initials as your name offers a kind of 'swagger'—linguistically."

"OK? But…"

"Nevermind, Ellen. Let's just get to it. I'm here to help. But you have to believe that I can."

"But I don't know you."

"By God, you do."

"Huh?"

"You know me by that name: God."

"You've got to be kidding?"

"Hey, I kid a lot, but not about who I am. Actually there are pretty dicey stories over the years about my sensitivity on that subject, but therapy's helping," he said and proceeded to start a nearby shrub on fire with a wink.

"Oh, my God!"

"Bingo! Now you're talkin'. And thanks for the greeting. But don't worry about the shrub; it will be fine. I was just proving my identity with a little theatrics."

"You're welcome?"

He continued. "Here's the thing: you forget you're not in charge. You're worried about what you did in the past; you regret what you did and what you didn't do. You figure if you do "the right thing," say "the right words," share the right "Dear Abby" columns time after time that your family will shape up to be who you think they should be. Trouble is, you can't figure out what the right thing to do or say or offer is. Plus, you can't seem to please anyone; they're annoyed with your concern and efforts; you hate what you're doing; and, despite all your efforts, no one is any closer to behaving in the 'right' way. Am I correct?"

"Yes. Spot on. I just can't figure out what to do."

"Hey, haven't you heard? If all you do is do and do and do, guess what you create? Lots of…."

Before he could finish His joke, He was laughing but noticed that I wasn't.

"OK, well, why can't you just "be."

"'Be' what?"

"Who you are."

"Oh, please. How will that help them?"

"Well, you'll be happier and you'll be out of my way. No offense, but it's difficult to get a word or action in edgewise when you're involved."

Not listening, I confessed, "God, they lied. Over and over. And they swore, over and over that they were OK. And I believed them. Or wanted to, chose to. They made such lousy choices in friends, developed horrible habits. I'm so embarrassed and ashamed to share the details."

"No need, Ellen; remember: I already know."

"God, I just feel so stupid. And so sad. And angry all at once." I sighed. "I just gotta face it; things just didn't work out."

"You sure about that? How would you know?"

"Well, look at their lives. My God…oh, excuse me; I guess I shouldn't use that expression with You. But, since I did, and since You are 'my God,' I guess You already know that I don't know; You're right."

"Me? Right? Ya think? Nice of you to consider it."

Ignoring His sarcasm, I continued, "But how shall I behave with them now? How do I know they're not still lying to me. And what if I'm contributing, yet again, to their lousy choices by loving them and helping them and being nice."

"What's your alternative?"

"Insist they leave, lock the doors, and forget they exist or are related to me."

"Think you can do that?"

"What?"

"Abandon them."

"I don't know, but maybe they'll learn something."

"And maybe they'll die."

"Die? Oh, my God; don't say that." I caught myself again using his name without thinking; the lapse made me laugh and consider another possibility. So I said, "But then again, if they die from my abandonment, at least they're Yours at that point! If I give up; You'll take them." I found myself smiling at the cavalier attitude I'd just projected.

But it was God's turn to be serious: "You know I will take them and care for them. But before I do, I'll let life teach them—maybe some really hard lessons—before I give them another life in which they'll learn more. And I'll love them throughout all eternity no matter what happens to them or what they do in each of those lives."

"But how can you do that--let them learn on their own like that."

"Dunno. It's just my way to get out of their way until they're ready. Confucius say, 'When the learner is ready, the teacher appears'; you know that. At least I think it was Confucius. My advice is simple: 'Control nothing. Enjoy everything. Love everyone.' And say nice things about Me, now and then. And a 'thank you' wouldn't hurt My feelings either."

"I wish I could live like that. It's just so difficult for me to let go of the worry and the responsibility and…."

"The control? It will help, as I said earlier, to realize that you have none. Control, that is. Let Me be in charge. I'm good at it. And wouldn't you like to rest awhile? You've got to be exhausted, trying to manage all your people and their circumstances. Let go, Ellen. Leave them in My care. It was never My intention for you to direct, guide, and control them. That's My role. Yours was to love, protect, and teach. You've done that; they were never yours to keep. They belong to Me, and I know what's best for them. You cannot love them into the life I want for them. Only I can do that. Your life is too brief to spend so much of it in fear and worry.

"Get out of their way. Let them go so that they can be themselves, whoever that may be. Plus, if you entrust them to Me, you will grow; and you will find the peace you want. Remember this: everything will be all right in the end. If it's not all right; it's not the end."

And with that, I heard the thunder and felt a few drops of rain hit my nose and cheeks. I turned my head at the sudden crack and flash of lightning over the next set of hills. When I turned again, I realized He was gone. Or I awoke. I'm still not sure.

What I do know for sure is that I want to return to the stroke of serenity I felt in those moments with Him. My path to serenity is giving up the fairy tale that I caused anyone else's problems, have any control over them, or can fix them. "Thy will be done" is my mantra and assures the serenity I seek. Living my own life in joyful celebration of each moment is my mission.

"Thank you, God. Nice work." Amen.

Ellen Peterson, 2013

*E*llen Peterson has worked as an employment counselor, a community organizer, and a media liaison for businesses, organizations, and individuals. A self-professed "matchmaker," she enjoys getting to know the passions, talents, and skills of those she is called on to showcase and promote in order to connect them with others who value what they can offer to a project or job. "Find a job you love," she offers, "and you'll never work a day in your life."

Essence of Sentience

Eyes see
Ears hear
Though we are more concerned right now
With what our I's are speaking –

You sprawl in resignation
Having heard the un-thoughts

From a distance of mere steps
Each length of which is vast

We both, I think, would like
The truth of touch
To amplify the conversation,
Though volume is futility.

The vet has chosen to restrain
-we both know you
aren't going anywhere-
because I mentioned you had snapped at me:
I meant to tell your depth of pain, but she heard only danger.

Here we are:

The nurse wields the syringe
That will separate
You from the pain

And me

-we both know you

Are going anywhere-

I lack the force to speak

To you   Or her.

Stop! For a moment.   Let me tell my pup

Good-bye! No time at all required. Just a single stroke

Above the site of the injection.

"I hope you heard me scream, and wish you well…"

Philip E. Repko

Vicarious Euphoria

Even after fifteen years of observation

We barely grasp the scope and weight

Of whirls, and flips, and twirls

Upon a four-inch beam.

Subjective scoring notwithstanding –

We are not shy

About assigning our own weightless grades.

We focus more on what we can assess:

Courage in reporting for duty

Freshman year,

Aware that balance due exceeded
All capacity to pay.

Grit in facing down a planned attack
When drunken guest confronts
A coed in a bathroom
In a near-deserted dorm.

Resolve in eagerly attacking
Morning training, evening practice –
Trying by example to exhibit
What commitment means.

And now, a final chance,
In hot pursuit of a fourth straight
National championship
Our daughter anchors the balance beam…

She knows this is her swan song,
We can tell. Everything on stage
Is made of tempered steel
(Except a threadbare shoulder joit.)

The floor, the vault, the bars
Have all concluded, leaving
Her alone on stage, the only
Lady left to ply the trade.
The crowd is quiet, waiting
As the day draws to a close.

To us, the time seems liquid,

Dripping lightly, seconds ooze.

And then, the end is here,

And we are beaming through the tears.

Astute judges post a score of 9.925,

A fourth improvement on a record.

But more importantly, to her,

The score ensures the title

For her team.   And we are awed

Again, but for the final time…

by Philip E. Repko

*P*hil Repko is a career educator in the PA public school system who has
been writing for fun and no profit since he was a teenager. Phil lives
with his wife Julie in Gilbertsville and is the father of three outstanding
children, two of whom are also poets and writers. He vacillates between
poetry and prose, as the spirit beckons, and is currently working sporadically
on a novella and a memoir.

Family Matters

I've learned to live in tides
That shift my heart now
In…then out…
And bring me back again.

I've learned to love the weightless floating
Touching softly shells that pass my hand in journeys I can't see.

My treasures won't be held too long. They cry,

"Let go. Let go.
"We must be free to drift and change and leave."

I weep but I let go.

I've learned to trust that glory will return and wear a different face.
The shell I loved will take its beauty far
And won't come home again.

Another Joy will take its place.
Each and each give transitory peace
And grief
When I let go…let go.

I've learned to live in flux.
And cry.
And laugh.

I've learned to let life go.

Jane Stahl, 1992

It's Spring

Summertime
by Ed McCarty

Come again, spring thaw.

Melt frozen dreams for bare feet

Racing back to life.

Jane Stahl, 2013

Jane Stahl currently serves as Director of Community Relations for Studio B following 35 years of sharing a love of literature, writing, and speaking with junior high and high school students and a love of teaching with fellow teachers and the community. Following their dream of living in an artistic community, Jane and her husband Paul founded Boyertown's Bear Fever community art project that ultimately led her into collaboration with fine artist Susan Biebuyck and the establishment of Studio B. So many projects, so little time! Jane hopes someday to take the time to self-publish a collection of her thoughts and experiences.

Bittersweet Vision

You find yourself in a cruel waiting game,
with words from a stranger you're never the same.
While in a trance, this downturn of fate,
out of the blue comes a new mental state
A powerful gift, this essence of fear,
strips down to the real and all becomes clear

You'll know where the love is, now easily seen,
the hearts that will lend a shoulder to lean.
The beauty of nature comes real beyond real,
a bittersweet gift found in the ordeal.

the mighty will weep,
the wise never knew,
the rich losing money
the brave become blue
the ironic truth
suddenly awakens,
that the truly alive
had everything taken.

Sharing this vision could change the world's fate.
It's a shame when it's found, that the hour is late.
If you pass through this enlightening flame,
and with words from a stranger, gone from whence it came,
remember that state as if woke from a dream,
in hopes you don't lose the real world you've seen.

You with post trauma, can now stop in awe,

At the sight of those warriors, that still see what you saw.

November

A blinded heart beats in the dark

Innocent love dimmed to exist

Like lighters that would only spark

Dark again and sorely missed

Such things did die but linger still

Summers passed and fall has flown

Possess the sky in winter chill

But only older I have grown

Yet vapors breath is slow to fleet

Desires ache and touch within

When chills on flesh rush body heat

I close my eyes let moonlight in

I breathe the air November night

Your soul goes racing through my heart

Your light skin joins emerging light

To blanket me as night clouds part

Maple
by Carrie Keplinger, 2012

In the late 80's and early 90's Burton was the lyricist-poet for the experimental industrial group "Slavekind." In his travels he met the world renowned electronic instrument designer Phillip Cirocco, Arizona avante-garde jazz bassist Gary Evans, and Michael Macdonald, former drummer of the group "Gene Loves Jezebel" from Scotland. This became the touring group "National Razor." Burton was lyricist for their four subsequent album releases. He also continued live reading performances. He was never content to write strictly about personal feelings although it was a great self-therapy. Consequentially, he turned from inward to outward on the many lessons and pathways in the world he was traveling. His latest endeavor is a collection of writings in the forthcoming book entitled <u>Beauty Among Thorns</u>.

Be Your Self
by Susan Biebuyck

Missing Link

Man loves woman. The two intertwine;
A child is conceived. Their love is combined.
"It's a girl!" A daughter, the missing link;
The two became three . . . a family sync.

What a lovely daughter, she deserves the best.
The finest of everything, she deserves nothing less.
But reality sets in and the rent needs to be paid;
Heat, food, clothes . . . there are sacrifices made.

All for the daughter, she'll never know;
How much was sacrificed for her to grow.
The two became a Mom and Dad.
They gave her the best of all they had.

The family of three was a bond unbroken;
Day in, day out, a love unspoken;
A chain of togetherness with just three links;
The two became three . . . a family sync.

Missing Link - 2 -

A new dress is needed, Mom works overtime;
The labor of love that she doesn't mind.
Daughter's hot in a dorm room and 2 hours away;
Dad shows up with a fan the very same day.

The cycle continues, Daughter's needs are fulfilled.
Mom and Dad's sacrifices are all free-willed.

Then one day . . .
There's a sacrifice calling, one they've known but ignored;
One that would take away the one they adored.
Daughter's engaged and plans to move away;
Mom and Dad's hearts say, "No! I want her to stay."

What happened to the family of three? The bond unbroken.
Day in, day out, a love unspoken;
A chain of togetherness with just three links;
The two became three . . . a family sync.

Missing Link - 3 -

Daughter marries and moves away, the chain is broken.
Day in, day out, heartbreak unspoken;
A chain of togetherness with a missing link;
Three minus one . . . no family sync.

Then one day . . .
An announcement is made: Daughter's having a child.
Mom and Dad are excited, they're hearts running wild.
"It's a boy!" A grandson, the missing link;
The four became five . . . a family sync.

The family of five was a bond unbroken;
Day in, Day out, a love unspoken;

A chain of togetherness, adding every child as a link;

Stretching across the miles . . . a lovely family sync.

Pamela M. Tuck

*P*amela Tuck is an award-winning children's book author. She was inspired to become a writer after her grandfather, the storyteller in the family, captivated her with his tales. When she was a child, Tuck remembers entertaining her family by recording her own voice and telling "made up silly stories." She won her first poetry contest in elementary school and continued to write short stories and plays. Most of Tuck's ideas come from her family and life experiences. She says, "I have such a rich family history.... It seems that there's not enough room for it all on paper." Pamela is the author of <u>As Fast As Words Could Fly</u>, <u>Color Struck</u>, and <u>The Adventure of Sheldon the Mushroom</u>. She lives with her husband and eleven children in Boyertown, PA.

Lost Hopes

I cry every morning when I drive to work. Usually, I can hold it together throughout the day and especially when I am around others, but when I am alone with my thoughts in my car, I cry.

This morning, though, I sobbed, as the empty ache consumed me and the weekend's events tumbled through my mind.

Yesterday, I found the strength and courage to go to the birthday party for my best friend's two-year-old son. These days, I felt sad and deprived to be around little children, let alone their happy families. But, for my friend, I came, smiled and talked.

I should have followed my plan and left early, but I stayed to watch little Josh open his presents. Biting my lip and trying to smile, I hoped no one noticed the tears in my eyes, as he happily tore through the wrapping paper.

The last present was a small box with a note from mom and dad.

"Surprise Josh, you are going to be a big brother," his dad announced, beaming as he read the note for everyone.

As the group of friends and family responded with congratulations and hugs, the tears started pouring down my face.

I can't be selfish and ruin this moment for them. Smile, smile. Say congratulations, I am so happy for you. Oh, I can't do this.

I look at Tom, who already had his arm around me and was pulling me to the back of the room.

"I have to go," I say. He nods and leads me toward the door and we head to the car.

"Wait here, I will be right back." And, he heads inside to explain and say goodbye.

I sob hysterically, feeling empty and alone.

Our children would have been the same age. They would have grown up as friends, maybe best friends, like Kate and me. We had known each other since we were 13 years old and wore braces. During high school, we worked together at the same ice cream store. We spent weeks at the beach during the summer, getting tan and sharing our secrets.

I hit the brake, as the yellow light turns red, and a mother and two toddlers cross the street in front of me.

Does everyone have children? Will I?

We waited to share the news with our friends and family until

I was in my third month, a safe time, we thought.

My mind plays the reel of events, from the first moment I got sick and thought I had the flu to the doctor's visit. I see the doctor's blank, composed face, as he tries to find a heartbeat with the ultrasound.

I enter the parking garage and turn left to go down the ramp and then turn right to pull into my space by the wall. As I turn off the engine, I look at my red, puffy face in the mirror. I pull out the makeup wipes from my purse and start wiping my eyes to prepare my face for the day.

Diane VanDyke, 2013

Parent Pride

The room grew silent as he stepped up to the podium to speak. I held my breath, not knowing what he would say or how he would do speaking for the first time in front of almost 80 friends and relatives.

Within a minute after he started talking—thanking his mentors, acknowledging the past help from his teachers and praising his friends—I relaxed and found myself smiling with pride. Sitting next to me, my daughter took photos with her iPhone.

As I looked at the young man in front who just received his pin for his Eagle Scout award, I could barely believe he was our son. He stood there so naturally, casually talking about his scouting experiences like he was sitting at our kitchen table.

I was wrong again, I thought. I argued and pleaded with him yesterday to take some note cards so he wouldn't forget what to say or at least to keep his thoughts organized.

"Mom, that's not me. I know what I will say in my head," he said, firmly opposing my suggestion of any type of written preparation.

"But, you might forget to thank someone or your mind may go

blank," I responded, insisting he take at least one card with some notes.

I lost the argument, and watching him now, I am glad I did.

My children over the years have taught me many things, from humility to simply looking at things from a different perspective. Life is not a matter of clear-cut rules—it has many exceptions, surprises and unexpected twists and turns.

Almost two decades ago, I thought I might never have children. Now, here I am in the midst of this scouting ceremony, feeling very proud of my children as they grow into adulthood. They are the joy of my life, and I love spending time with them and being an active part of their busy lives.

As the ceremony continued with its formalities, my mind drifted to a story I once read or heard about how our lives are like quilts. We only see the underside of the quilt, with its many tangled, knotted threads. What we don't see or know is the beautiful pattern that has been created on the top.

As I watched our son shake hands and accept congratulations, I think of all those threads, those myriad moments of teaching, prodding and shaping that lead to moments like this, when we can get a glimpse of the amazing design being formed.

Diane VanDyke, 2013

Whether she is writing a journal entry or an article for a local newspaper, Diane VanDyke finds her creative zone when she connects words and phrases to paint a lasting image and tell a good story. Her writing adventures started in her teenage years but then were put aside and rediscovered a decade later when she started freelance writing for her hometown newspaper. Her freelance assignments led to a part-time staff position and then to a full-time editorial position. Eventually, she followed the path of marketing and public relations, where she currently uses her writing skills today. Beyond writing, Diane likes to garden, hike, jog, read, ride bike and enjoy the beauty of sunrises and sunsets.

Stillness
by Lauralynn White, 2013

Forty-Four

All was Bliss

(And Struggle).

I was not worthy; yet, I was one with my beloved.

I was loved.

It was ALL.

I was vile and at loose ends.

I tortured that which I most adored and desired to be near.

By the imperfection and disease of my soul I drove my love away.

All was dark/black and filled with eternal infinite pain.

I renounced my beloved and was alone.

Joy departed.

I was filled with (nothing but) despair unseen.

I lived. How was it that I lived?

Without, Purged, Bereft, Alone I waited.

I waited…I waited…

In complete stillness an answer comes: Hope.

Hope that I will yet become what I was not.

Compassionate, Even-keeled, Peaceful, Without Need, Whole.

I am transformed by gratitude for the gift given by the beloved.

All is Bliss.

Lauralynn White, 2013

*L*auralynn White is an artist pursuing her own vision of the world. She is a graduate of Savannah College of Art and Design with a BFA in Illustration and Art History. She is a juried member of the National Association of Women Artists, as well as a juried Studio Artist and the Gallery Director at GoggleWorks Center for the Arts. She is an exhibiting artist at Studio B, Boyertown, PA and Visual Arts Chautauqua Institution. She has participated in various national and international exhibits and has been a juror for Albright University and York Arts. Her first solo exhibition, "Figurescapes" was named in the Top Ten of 2012 in Visual Arts by the Reading Eagle.

Lauralynn notes that the poem is "rooted in Sufi thought. A religious piece, it's an exposition of the direction and meaning of her figurescapes. It's also a declaration of the journey taken by many which includes an estrangement from the Creator and our need to reconcile ourselves in order to come into the presence of God. To stop seeking/striving and just to be who we are in our souls. It has taken me seven years to understand this enough to write down this small offering. And I could not have written it sooner."

Ancient Injury

In the evenings, he would read to me or we would tell stories about when we were children, living in towns not far from the one another. They were usually funny stories, but some involved moments wherein the soul of the other was revealed in sacred exchanges.

As a boy, he had made and played with bows and arrows, aiming at targets of all kinds. Once, he saw a small owl, was able to sneak up on it and snap an arrow off the bow at close range. He wasn't prepared for what happened next. The arrow went into the bird, and a drop of blood appeared on the white breast feathers. The bird's bright eyes fixed on him, and blinked once before it fell over. His boy's heart pounded, as a feeling came over him he had never experienced. He and the beautiful living creature had been so close they breathed the same air, and then it was gone, but not the image of fixed eyes nor the memory of awakening his conscience as sharply and unexpectedly as a deadly arrow.

There was another story he told once, and only once—of an experience leaving an even deeper imprint. As a marine in Vietnam, where one was always in danger, vigilant for snipers and hiding places from which anyone could and did spring at any moment (for such is the nature of war), he noticed a strange area on the ground ahead, and a heard a movement. A part of the terrain had been disturbed, and a dug out spot covered over. Not taking any chances, he fired his rifle into the opening. As the other members of the detail gathered round, they looked in and saw bodies. They helped him pull them out by their ankles—two women, whose weight he feels still. His fellow Marines thanked him for saving their lives, and later he received a medal for his deed. He never showed it to anyone, except once to me, then hid it away as he had the faces of the dead women.

Nothing could ever change what happened that day he had set out a young man and returned that night as something else he could never again quite recognize, so he didn't look. But some images never fade; we all have our precious store of sorrow to stare into, and the ways we learn to blot them out, avoid them, tuck them safely away, or bear them only inwardly—thorns piercing us with shame and regret, even when we aren't looking. Then, at unexpected times without warning, those images loom up before us in a dream or a memory. If we are lucky, we have someone to hold us in silence.

That is what true lovers have ever done when a sacred exchange has taken place. They silently give over to the others' innermost being. Even if unaware of, or unfamiliar with that innermost part, each asking the other to protect and nurture it throughout all time.

Willy is my child; he is my father
I would be his lady all my life.
He said he'd love to live with me
But for an ancient injury which has not healed

(Joni Mitchell)

Sandra Williams, 2001

Illustration by Robert Williams ,1969

*S*andra taught world literature and writing at both the high school and higher education levels since earning a BA in English and Secondary Education at Ursinus College and an MA in English at Villanova University . She is a writer of poetry, essays and short stories, with several published articles. She has been associated with Studio B since 2010 offering various adult writing opportunities. Sandra believes writing is both therapeutic and enlightening—as "if we become aware of what inspires us, expand our imagination, delve into our own knowledge and experience, and rely on our intuitive selves." She collaborates with her husband, Robert, local landscape and mural painter, promoting community arts. www.cosmicseanotes. blogspot.com

www.ingramcontent.com/pod-product-compliance
Lightning Source LLC
Chambersburg PA
CBHW021911040426
42447CB00007B/812